Railways in Your Garden

RAILWAYS
IN YOUR
GARDEN

Edited by
David Pratt & David Joy

GardenRail - 1994

GardenRail, P.O. Box 42, Skipton, North Yorkshire, BD23 5UZ

ISBN: O 9523766 0 1

First published 1994

Published in association with Garden Railway Specialists,
Station Studio, Princes Risborough, Bucks, HP27 9DT

Design and layout: Trevor Ridley

Printed in Great Britain

Contributors:

Michael Adamson
David Gray
David Joy
David Pinniger
Becky Pinniger
David Pratt
Derek Shephard

Front cover photograph of the Schmalspurbahn Walchensee by Len Rosier

Picture credits:- Michael Adamson and collection: Pages 16, 23, 27, 48 (bottom), 50, 51 (top), 52, 56, 57, 66, 71; David Edgley: 62, 63; David Gray: 41, 58, 61, 68; David Joy: 33, 45, 67, 72, 73, 76, 78; David Pinniger: 15, 46, 47, 48 (top), 51 (bottom), 53, 70, 74; John Whisson: 9, 12, 13, 19, 20, 25, 30, 32, 36, 37, 40, 44, 45, 55, 60, 65, 69, 76.

Drawing on page 8 by permission of Brandbright Ltd.

Contents

Introduction

To newcomers, welcome to one of the most satisfying and diverse hobbies that it is possible to find. To old hands, we hope to give you inspiration and new encouragement. Recently, big-scale modelling has developed rapidly. This is leading to more and cheaper models and accessories, which in turn results in lower prices generally.

Garden railways complement the small indoor scales and for many provide an unexpected development when suddenly the whole family becomes involved. On a track that is fully integrated into your garden, it is possible to run different types of rolling stock, whether old-time American, European or British. These can be in different scales, and powered by different means. Each member of your family can be responsible for his/her own area of interests whether this is a live-steam locomotive, radio-controlled models, model buildings and construction or horticulture.

The hobby can also incorporate electronics and civil engineering. Under construction in a garden as this book is written is a twenty-foot replica of the Forth Bridge. A twelve-foot long suspension bridge across a river, held up by bicycle chains, is already taking daily traffic on the Meon Valley Light Railway.

We will not forget those who build a complete layout on their patio or in a small garden and still have space to sit and watch the trains go by.

The biggest difference for most railroaders is that they are operating in the real world - rain, snow and leaves will all fall, whilst hedgehogs and frogs will hibernate in tunnels. These hazards all make railway operations more like the real thing, and with an extended layout you may even need "staff" to clear the track, tend the landscape or drive drains, switch points and operate signals.

Garden railways have existed in the U.K. for over fifty years and in Europe since the 1960s with the advent of Lehmann-LGB G-Scale, from

Germany. In the past decade the U.S.A. has begun to demand and produce more and more products as the hobby has developed.

The aim of this book is to provide a general source and reference work into which you can dip, as your knowledge and your layout grow, for inspiration, information and enjoyment. So, whether the attraction is those big model locomotives, watching the trains go by, or landscaping in miniature, we hope that you will find something of interest on every page, and return time and time again to these words and ideas from some of the most experienced garden railway modellers.

If you have not done so already, you should acquire as many catalogues as you can, and visit your nearest shop that has comprehensive stocks.

The most basic models come from Playmobil, which uses LGB track, and from Bachmann, which models more realistically. Either will get you started very cheaply. A small amount of these products - a battery-powered diesel locomotive or a simple radio-controlled (battery-powered) old time steam set can provide an excellent and interesting beginning. This also provides play opportunities for unsupervised children and for friends, even when your track is permanently in place and you have moved on to better things.

The American Bachmann company produce a very realistic basic train and circle of track including batteries with radio control, at a price comparable to Playmobil, which is more toy like and found in better toy shops. The catalogues will tell you more, and the all important prices. At least one specialist dealer publishes a frequent newsletter listing secondhand equipment.

A good first read is the catalogue from Lehmann, who produce LGB (Lehmann GrossBahn). They have been the in the G-Scale railway business since the 1960s and are generally regarded as the best for quality and range of their products. Most manufacturers try to be compatible with LGB. The Walthers large scale book (it IS a book) is a giant catalogue that lists almost everything available anywhere and comes from the U.S.A.

It is difficult if not impossible to determine why railways, especially steam ones, hold such a fascination. Whatever the reason, it affects old and young alike. Model trains have become more and more realistic and sophisticated in operation, culminating in the modern garden railway - probably the closest you can come to the real thing!

SCALES

Garden railways have been built in many scales over the last seventy years or so. Common scales in use include Gauge 0 (1:43) popularised by Hornby and Bassett Lowke in clockwork and electric forms; and Gauge 1 (1:32) which has even older roots in Marklin, Carette and Bing. Both of these scales model standard gauge railways.

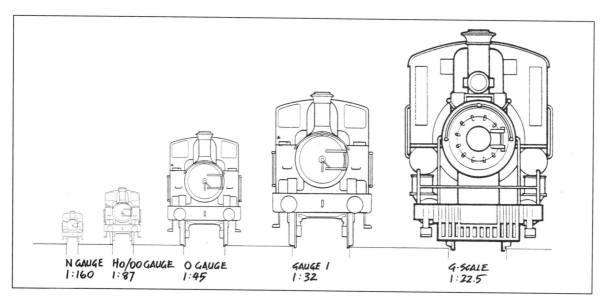

N GAUGE 1:160   HO/OO GAUGE 1:87   O GAUGE 1:45   GAUGE 1 1:32   G-SCALE 1:22.5

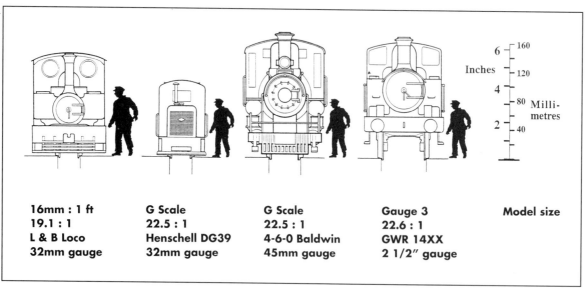

16mm : 1 ft
19.1 : 1
L & B Loco
32mm gauge

G Scale
22.5 : 1
Henschell DG39
32mm gauge

G Scale
22.5 : 1
4-6-0 Baldwin
45mm gauge

Gauge 3
22.6 : 1
GWR 14XX
2 1/2" gauge

Model size

6 — 160
Inches
4 — 120
— 80   Milli-
— metres
2 — 40

In 1967 E. P. Lehmann Patentwerk of Nuremburg introduced Lehmann Grossbahn (LGB) with a track gauge the same as gauge 1 (45mm) and a scale of around 1:22.5 modelling narrow gauge prototypes. Recently this has assumed the title of G scale with the introduction of several new manufacturers who in turn have produced variations of the quoted scale.

There are similarities between G scale and 16mm scale both of which model narrow gauge prototypes. However, the latter runs on 32mm gauge track and has a scale of 1:19. G scale prototypes are metre, three foot or three foot-six gauge, occasionally two foot-six. 16mm prototypes are nominally two foot gauge.

This well integrated railway shows in the foreground an LGB Mallet (a large articulated narrow gauge locomotive) with working lights and smoke generator. in the middle distance is the LGB "White Pass" diesel from the Yukon, Alaska — which still runs today. High up in the background an old timer from the U.S.A. crosses an authentic trestle bridge. The track, figures and girder bridge are LGB and the tunnel mouth is from Garden Railway Specialists, as is the trestle bridge

1
Getting started

You've decided that you want to enter the world of big model railways, so where do you go from here? At the risk of stating the obvious, the first and most important point to bear in mind is not to let your hobby take over to the point where it ceases to be fun. Each one of us has his or her preferences. The whole of this book is not, generally speaking, going to tell you to do anything, except when it comes to safety aspects. The aim is to feed you with ideas, so that you are stimulated into making choices which suit the way that YOU want to go with your railway, and to develop it to suit your own particular style and need. We are however, going to concentrate on what have become known as the scenic scales - G scale and 16mm - and on lines integrated with the garden.

Most of us have started in the same way, with the cheapest available locomotive, probably a diesel shunter (switcher) and one wagon plus a piece of track. All that we could do initially was run the locomotive up and down this short length of track, probably with a battery connected to the rails. Exciting at first because of the size and realism. We all tired of this and looked to the great outdoors and getting something running in the garden.

The point here is this - not many of us are millionaires, but even if you do have plenty of spare cash, it pays to start simply, and gradually develop your rolling stock, your line and your ideas, learning from your experiences and your mistakes as you go along.

A BEGINNING – MINIMUM REQUIREMENTS

The absolute minimum is not much more than described above. You will need some track, something to run on it and a power unit to make it all work. Of course, you will be itching to see the train running, so at an early stage you should decide what style of layout you are going to build. Layout designs are discussed in a later section, but you should plan so that initial trackwork can be put down fairly quickly, in such a way that running can commence and maintain your interest. Yet you need to consider how the layout will develop as time and money permit, unlike the railroader who spent two years laying track and has not turned a wheel - he wondered why he was losing interest!

We would suggest initially, either an end to end line or a simple circuit. This will be influenced by the shape of your garden, and how the various features such as lawns, rockeries or flower beds already make up its structure.

If you opt for end to end, then remember that you will be constantly starting and stopping the train, unless the line is long. Being your own engine driver may be fun to start with, and we know of a number of railway modellers who love shunting operations, but you might tire of it eventually. However, there is an advantage with this type of layout in that it will impinge less on the existing framework of the garden, especially with a line laid alongside paths, lawns or flower beds. There are reversing units, some built into buffers, and these will be described later.

If you want things really simple, then all you need initially for motive power is a tram or a railcar. These need no wagons or carriages to haul, and so do not need points for running around at terminals, although sidings will be needed with your next rolling stock purchases.

Opting for a circular or rather a continuous layout will probably make more demands on your creative ability to integrate the railway into garden features. A continuous run does have advantages though because it allows

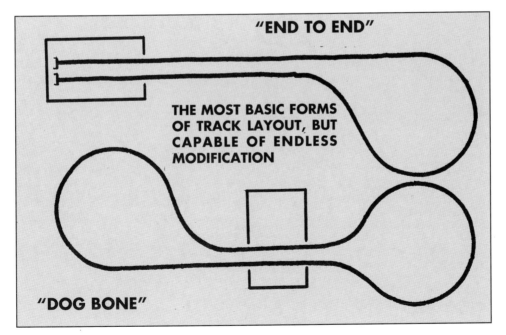

"END TO END"

THE MOST BASIC FORMS OF TRACK LAYOUT, BUT CAPABLE OF ENDLESS MODIFICATION

"DOG BONE"

It is not necessary to buy a large amount of rolling stock and locomotives, track and accessories to start garden railroading. One vehicle, such as the Delton Doozie Railcar, a circle of track in the rockery and a few passengers will provide stimulation and interest, and this always leads on to bigger things

you to start up a train and just let it run while you relax, watch it and plan the next development - or possibly even do some gardening!

If all this sounds rather basic, the scenic scales are of such a size and presence that once you get out of doors into the sunlight, then no matter how simple the layout, or how limited the rolling stock, it looks real, just like the prototype. Which leads us on to ....

THE REAL THING

Models of narrow gauge railways can offer you the world, because the prototypes have so much variety. A train can consist of a single railcar, a

Still under construction but taking fast goods traffic already, an elevated section of track leads onto a rockery via a massive LGB girder bridge. The track support of timber on timber posts will disappear beneath ballast and will be planted underneath with privet and climbers around the posts. The newly laid track on the rockery is on a cement bed. The rockery and track bed areas were allowed to settle and consolidate for a season before the railway engineering works began. This is especially important where bridge abutments are involved to prevent settling after the track is in place

steam, diesel or electric locomotive pulling or pushing one or two coaches with perhaps a van at the back for goods or parcels. At the other end of the spectrum we can have a modern locomotive hauling over a dozen coaches or wagons. The permutations are endless. There are in existence around the world narrow gauge systems with the latest technology, electric locomotives and all the panoply of a mainline system which rival the very best that standard gauge has to offer. Equally there are ancient steam locomotives, weed-covered track, rickety railbuses or hybrid systems that start off as city tramways and end up as country branch lines.

This is the beauty of our scales. You will be able to chose the type of line you want to run in your garden, and very likely be able to purchase ready-made models to suit. If you feel like creating your own models, a vast array of parts is available for scratchbuilding. Or you can always modify that old Playmobil or Bachmann that got you started. There are brave modellers who modify LGB despite the cost.

There is also great satisfaction in moulding a tunnel mouth with modelling clay, and casting this via a latex mould in quick setting cement, to suit that particular need of your railway.

KEEPING THE AUTHORITIES HAPPY

We have already mentioned that garden railways usually involve the whole family. They will not appreciate, however, a building site that has replaced their favourite piece of lawn or flower bed. A railway on elevated wooden boards is arguably not a garden railway but a layout out of doors and this can often be a nuisance and an eyesore.

A garden railway should blend with and enhance the garden. There should be a reason for the tunnel or bridge in maintaining a level track despite the ups and downs of the terrain. Not only does this make the garden more pleasing to the eye but it helps to create a more realistic appearance. It will also draw other members of your family into taking an interest. While you are planning or building with a railwayman's eye, your partners can most certainly help and advise independently about gardening aspects.

Many happy hours can be spent at gardening centres, choosing suitable heathers, ground cover plants, alpines or dwarf conifers to complement the railway. It is possible to make the whole of the lineside a herb garden since most of these attractive plants have small leaves and flowers in scale with the passing trains. Watching plants mature over the years as the railway also slowly develops is a most satisfying part of the hobby.

When you are planning your line, and assuming that you are to have conventional electrically-powered traction, you can certainly allow for some gradients, but we suggest not steeper than one in forty. Many models have a rubber traction tyre on the wheels to assist with grip on gradients. All locomotives rely on their weight for grip in real life. Allowing for some minor gradients and the need for a bridge or tunnel for variety, you should be able to follow the contours that exist.

The best angle from which to view your railway is about two feet above, with a lineside view now and then following our real life view at stations, or perhaps over a lineside fence. It is clearly impossible for most people to have their railways naturally elevated to three or four feet above the ground, and so compromises are required.

If your garden is more or less level then some gentle gradients will add interest. They will also make live steam engines work hard and so sound better. Often it is possible to dig a hole for a pond and use the spoil for an embankment though grass cutting could be a problem. (Camomile looks the part and covers the ground like moss).

Track construction and laying are covered elsewhere in this book, but bear in mind that firm foundations are vital. This is engineering for real! Try to avoid laying the track in dead straight lines, but instead follow gentle curves, complementing the shape of flowerbeds and so on, or creating new ones for the railway. Prototype narrow gauge lines are pretty sinuous anyway. After all, narrow gauge was chosen by engineers because of its flexibility in coping with gradients and dramatic landscape changes. A train will look more interesting if it is allowed to wind through the garden environment with light and shadow falling at different angles on locomotive and rolling stock.

MOTIVE POWER

Here we are talking about the method of propulsion for your models. In large-scale model railways you do have some choice in the matter, although the vast majority of G scale modellers use conventional electric power. That is, the mains feeding a transformer with the trains drawing up to twenty volts and two amps from the rails. This is a very reliable method over quite large distances, particularly if the pieces of track are bonded together electrically to reduce voltage drop and "dead" track. However, you must contrive to keep any mains cable indoors, and preferably with a sensitive circuit breaker at the live end.

Most models are weatherproof and to cater for masochists there are even snow ploughs on the market to keep your railway running in the most severe conditions!

Two-truck Shay ploughing the snow on David Pinniger's Burnham and Berkshire Railroad

When you begin to run more than one locomotive it will be necessary to provide isolating sections where you can switch off the track electricity. If you do not do this all the trains will begin to run at once as soon as current is fed to the line. One solution is to operate track powered and overhead powered trains together, but with separate power supplies. This could be achieved with only one controller but switched between the two possibilities.

Many locomotives actually have a switch or switches fitted whereby you can turn off the power to the wheels, leaving the lights or smoke generator on and combinations of these. Some locomotives also have the choice of track or overhead pick-up. Lastly, with an overhead pick-up layout it is simple to drop the overhead collector (pantograph) of any locomotive, to isolate it from the power supply.

Another form of motive power supply is the good old battery, rechargeable or otherwise. Some locomotives, particularly diesels, are bulky enough to accept a pack of ni-cad rechargeables or even sealed lead-acid moped/scooter batteries and a small controller operated by radio control. Pushed to the limit, you can even find space for the electronic sound generator and loudspeaker too! Alternatively, batteries can be located in a goods van and the current fed through to the locomotive via cables.

An attractive Continental-style layout in Germany, with a lot of railway in a relatively small space. The water in the centre makes a good focal point

2
Planning the Railway

Devising the plan is probably the most important activity of all. Hours, weeks and months spent on planning and designing a garden railway will always be well rewarded. The potential problems go far beyond those of an indoor layout in smaller scales, where it can be merely the case of seeing that curves and points will fit the space available. Outside, the frequent absence of any specific boundaries can make the number of possibilities so numerous that sometimes the newcomer simply does not know where to begin.

There is a great responsibility in the fact that you are creating something semi-permanent at least, and changing the real environment, so be sure that you are doing it for the better. Try in the first instance to take an overall view and decide which type of line will give the greatest satisfaction, not just to yourself but to the whole household. Garden railways used to be an all-male preserve, but this is no longer the case. The modern concept involves a line which, by careful planning and planting, provides a natural setting for the railway, and enhances rather than disfigures the surroundings of flower bed, rockeries or lawns. Finally, make sure that you can expand the layout if and when required.

PROTOTYPE OR FREELANCE?

Although the great outdoors might at first glance seem ideal to model a prototype station or section of a real line, this is in fact seldom the case. The sheer size of the models means that an enormous space is required and usually something gets in the way. Any slight departure from the real thing defeats the object of the exercise, and therefore most modellers opt for a freelance or "fun" railway. This can take on almost any form depending upon the personality of the operator.

Driver, signalman or constructor? Are you the sort of enthusiast who in imagination is firmly in the cab of the locomotive, following it round the layout as it constantly shunts and changes train make up? If so, a layout with several stations, goods depots or sidings will be required. Others dream of being signalmen, directing trains to the appointed place on the line or platform at the station. In which case, junctions, loops and multiple routing possibilities are likely to be favoured.

Then again, the spectator who is just happy to watch the trains go round will prefer a simple design with broad, sweeping curves. Lastly but by no means least, there will be many who wish to give movement and added interest as well as purpose to their garden for gardening's sake, providing an extra dimension to rockeries, alpines and dwarf planting and drawing together all the horticultural elements.

LAYOUT CHARACTER

There are many options here. The simplest layout of all, the continuous circuit, can work quite satisfactorily in the garden, where flowers and landscaping can easily disguise the circular nature. It is ideal for the spectator, and is also particularly suitable for live-steam operation. A variant, especially on sloping ground, is the dumb-bell or dog-bone shape.

An out-and-back system is easy for the single operator, although a relatively large space is needed for the turning circle. The "driver" may prefer end-to-end operation with the two termini close together if he is on his own or the space is limited. Separate termini are more authentic and give the greatest return in terms of train movements and types (no pun intended!).

The "signalman" will favour a combination of two or more of the above, which is perfectly feasible, perhaps working from a signal box in the garden shed. As with an indoor layout, it also helps if the line has a sense of purpose and credibility, an identity. Is it to be a main line carrying passenger and freight traffic, or a sleepy branch with mixed trains? Will it be in central Europe, the USA, South Africa? Will it be last century, the beginning of this or more recent still?

Then again, it could be industrial, serving a quarry or sawmill, and perhaps hauling real loads from one place to another. Or might it be more of a tramway? All of these considerations need careful thought, and only when firm conclusions have been reached should detailed planning begin.

SITE PLANNING

The shape, size and nature of the garden will have a fundamental bearing on the type of railway to be constructed. Some modellers with a new house can thus combine garden railway construction in a single garden laying

Though not strictly conforming to our garden railway definition of true integration with the surroundings, this line is raised above ground in a unique way for wheelchair observation. Access is also improved in the engine shed behind. When the climbers have finished growing up netting attached to the upright floor joists the effect will be softer. Thus the elevated track has become a feature

operation. More often we have an existing garden and certain constraints are imposed. This could be a stream or pond. Trees, especially, are immovable. Drives and pathways will present civil engineering problems if they are to be crossed. There are also hazards from trees that drop sticky resin, and areas of sun or shade may affect rail expansion.

Some modellers will be lucky enough to have an existing rockery, in many ways the perfect site; others may have a sloping site, also adding interest. The great majority of us, however, start with a flat site, mostly lawn.

This means that our most often encountered problem is one of track height. Ground level resembles a train set on the floor, and operation or maintenance can cause acute backache problems. On the other hand, too high an elevation involves costly and prodigious engineering works. There is also less chance of the line blending with the surroundings. One compromise is a rockery some two feet above a sunken lawn, and accessible at all points.

Operating pits, suitably drained, enable stock to be reached with ease. Another way is to excavate part of the site and use this material for a mound or rockery, put a pond in the hole and use the mound as a rockery base.

A ROOF FOR ALL SEASONS

Many garden railways start off with a simple open-air line, rolling stock being carried out of the house for each operating session and carried back again afterwards. Apart from the risk of damage from repeated handling, this can soon become a chore. It is far more satisfactory if the line can include a covered area which permits rolling stock to be kept dry when it rains. The undercover area can be part of the house car port, or garage. Greenhouses should be avoided because of the huge temperature variations and high humidity.

Another possibility is a free-standing shed, sited near the house for security reasons and fed with a mains supply, suitably protected. This shed may have to be sizeable. Scale trains can be up to fifteen feet long - and

Here a Lionel Atlantic (almost G Scale) pulling Bachmann wagons passes a pair of Aristo-Craft FA1 diesels running light from the garden shed, securely hidden in a corner of the garden. Note also the raised track level

more! Local regulations might have to be observed for a permanent brick-built structure. In any event, doors, windows and train access hatches must all be lockable. The shed can combine both termini of any end to end line or can be sited in the centre of a dog-bone shaped layout. It can also provide a site office during construction - somewhere to solder for instance.

LAYOUT PLANNING

With a decision on the concept and type of line, its position in the garden, and the most suitable home for the rolling stock, actual layout planning can now begin in earnest.

Start by making your sketches on paper. Keep it simple and assuming this is the more usual freelance line, remember that you are aiming for some fun rather than total authenticity. The bigger it is, the more it will cost to build and to maintain. Single track will be cheaper by half of course, and also gives a better illusion of distance.

Allow for future expansion. In devising the track plan there must be sufficient provision for shunting and for trains to pass each other, as well as stabling spare locomotives and rolling stock. Run-round loops should be long enough for the longest train that you can foresee to allow the locomotive to move from front to rear for its return journey. Buildings can take up a great deal of space, and you might need to provide scenery and extra planting.

At an early stage you will have to decide on the locations of tunnels, bridges, cuttings and embankments if they are not already forced upon you by the garden's topography. Tunnels should be viewed with great caution - Murphy's Law dictates that if anything is to go really wrong on a garden railway, it will do so in a tunnel. Any tunnel must be readily accessible, with the centre within an arm's reach.

When it comes to crossing pathways, ground level is preferable to a lifting section in an elevated track. "Bar flaps", sometimes disguised as a bridge that will lift out or hinge up, always require some clever electrical connections and security measures to avoid spectators lifting the track in the path of a train!

Cuttings too have their drawbacks, being damp and prone to landslips with difficult tracklaying and maintenance. They are also a collecting area for fallen leaves and any windblown rubbish. They are especially valued by garden animals as footpaths.

Curves and gradients are a key factor in your trackwork and also in giving realism. Those with indoor layouts will have to adjust from minimum radius thinking to always providing the maximum radius on curves. Think big! Try to use transitional curves following the practice for real tracks. This is the provision of a slightly larger radius curve leading into the smaller radius of the curve proper. In some cases a left-hand curve is made as the entry to a full right-hand curve. Long sweeping curves will give the best view of your trains in motion.

Flexible track is a great advantage and also a saving over sectional track with its preformed curves or short straights. It also gives fewer joints to bond. Similarly, nothing looks worse than sharp radius turnouts when there is all the space in the world and long wagons or locomotives are forced to overhang unrealistically or dangerously. There is always the temptation to use small radius points on cost grounds but you will almost always want to change to large radius as operational experience grows.

Many of the same principles apply to gradients. The desirable maximum gradient is about one in sixty for live steam and one in thirty for electric traction. With the latter, short trains hauled by a heavy engine (for better traction through its greater adhesion) can cope with one in twenty-five for short lengths, but this only increases wear and tear on the tracks and locomotives. This was also very common on main lines with real locomotives suffering from broken springs and worn bearings. Gradients should be the vertical equivalent of transitional curves, with a more gentle gradient leading into the incline proper. A severe incline in the middle of curves should also be avoided, or friction will add to the difficulties.

SURVEYING

After drawing and redrawing many plans on paper, the time will come to translate these into reality on the ground. Some modellers lay the track in rough position on mother earth and start digging. A more exact approach is usually preferable, particularly if you are opting for more permanent foundations. A combination of boards, stakes, spirit level and string is needed. A very useful device for levelling over large distances is a garden

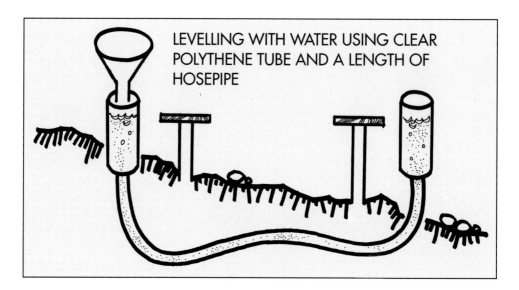

LEVELLING WITH WATER USING CLEAR POLYTHENE TUBE AND A LENGTH OF HOSEPIPE

hose with a length of clear tubing attached at each end. When this is filled with water, then wherever the two clear ends are the visible water level in them will be the same.

Straight and level track laying is easy enough. Simply lay a board on the ground and place the spirit level on top, excavating and infilling until the desired result is obtained. The "spoil" surplus is used to fill in hollows in just the same way as the navvies built the nineteenth century's vast railway networks. You are following in a long and honourable tradition.

Gradients require a little calculation. If a board one hundred units long is raised by one unit at one end you have a gradient of one in a hundred. Curves are measured and marked by driving a stick into the ground at the centre point of the desired curve. Attach a length of string to this and draw your giant circle just as you would with a compass.

There are almost as many different ways of track-laying as there are garden railways! Here is one approach, with the garden path sensibly being built at the same time

3
Trackwork

The largest expense at the beginning of your railway project will be the track itself. It is impossible to try to build a layout a metre at a time, so try to complete a section in one go. This will also assist with your electrical isolation and control later as well.

There are many types of track available. In G scale the 45mm gauge track can be divided into three basic types:

(a) Track completely compatible with LGB track, e.g. Bachmann, REA/Aristo, Playmobil, Lionel.

(b) Track only compatible with special joiners, e.g. Tenmille G scale, PECO G scale.

(c) Track that will not join to LGB because of totally different rail and sleeper measurements, e.g. Tenmille Gauge 1, Flatbottom or Bullhead.

LGB COMPATIBLE TRACKS

Lehmann (LGB) offers a very comprehensive track system, based upon sectional and flexible types. All rails are solid brass with plastic sleeper base fully detailed with woodgrain and chairs to hold the rails. This base is manufactured from BASF LURAN-S which is immensely strong and has good ultra-violet stability for out-of-doors use. Rail joiners are of brass or insulating plastic (coloured bright yellow). Apart from a vast catalogue of preformed track sections, with insulators, there are train detecting switches or magnets, diamond crossings and various points. Flexible track is also available in 1.5 metre lengths with separate fishplates.

Home-built points at the entry to a main station constructed about twelve inches above ground level. Sleepers are wood. These points are manually operated because the trains are all radio controlled with about 24 volts permanently supplied to the rails. Each "driver" can then deal exclusively with one train in response to the signals

Points - turnouts to the railwayman - are available from LGB in two radii. The smaller circle is sold by Playmobil as well at a slightly lower price. The larger radius turnout is always worth the extra investment. Both types can be operated by electric motors in weatherproof housings which also accept switch attachments and lanterns. The large range of track accessories, including uncouplers (automatic or fixed), buffers (with electronic reversers) and level crossing is detailed in a very readable and massive catalogue.

BACHMANN

This American company offers two types of track construction, both fully compatible with LGB. The first is metal sectional track, a hollow section of plated metal. This is just like pre-war Hornby "0" gauge track but mounted on a modern plastic sleeper base. Straights and curves are available. Outdoors it will presumably ultimately rust.

The second system is an all plastic variety which is lightweight and only suitable for battery-operated rolling stock. It can be used in indoor storage yards for cheapness.

RAILWAY EXPRESS AGENCY/ARISTO

This American G scale track is not widely available outside the USA. It has similar appearance to LGB, so much so that legal proceedings were started. A newer version, also available from Bachmann, has American spiked sleepers.

LIONEL

The Lionel system, available in all scales, has a brass "Bachmann like" G scale track but this time the rail joiners are non standard. A metal pin pushes into the hollow rail of the next section. The track is obviously lightweight and pins would need to be removed to join to other makes.

PLAYMOBIL

Manufactured in Germany by Lehmann and indistinguishable from LGB, this track is only available in the smaller sections with smaller radiuses but includes uncouplers, points and plastic buffer stops.

TENMILLE G SCALE

This British track is very close to LGB in appearance but has 40% less metal and so is considerably cheaper. The rail top and height are the same with the saving in the webb and base. The track is available in sectional or long flexible forms. The sleeper spacing is slightly different to LGB with one less per foot. There are converter fishplates to join the track to LGB which are black plastic with a removable metal insert for electrical continuity or isolation as needed. Brass rail joiners are fitted. It is necessary to cut the plastic joining the sleepers on the underside of the rail when bending the flexible track to a curve. There are very large radius points (1.6m) and kits available. These are also longer than LGB units and closer to prototypical practice.

PECO G45

Another well established British company, known for its range of scale trackwork. This track in G scale is somewhat different from the others that we have looked at previously. Whilst Peco have used a plastic base with the usual woodgrain effect, the spacing is considerably larger and irregular. This gives the effect of the so-called "crazy track" that is available from them in smaller scales. The idea is that it more closely follows British narrow gauge two-foot prototypes.

The rail profile is smaller than LGB rail and sits lower. Thus it needs to be raised if there is a transition to another make. A special joiner is available. The track is also available in aluminium or nickle silver - slightly more expensive. Aluminium is not recommended out of doors where a film of insulating oxide forms, although it has been used in drier climates than the British Isles, with some success.

The track is available in sectional and one-yard length flexible forms, points in nickel silver only, rail-built buffer stops and a special point motor.

NON LGB COMPATIBLE SYSTEMS

In this category we are considering various 10mm scale track systems, which will accept all modern LGB and other rolling stock, with a few provisoes, manufactured by firms such as Tenmille. The tracks are usually designed for gauge 1, with a sleeper spacing more in keeping with main line standards. Sleepers can be plastic or wooden, usually with integrally moulded chairs for the plastic variety. Chairs for wooden sleepers are usually plastic with a small spigot that pushes into a hole drilled in the sleeper. Rail profiles can be flat-bottomed or bullhead. Fishplates are available and the rail is nickel silver or brass.

The pleasing effect of large radius points, including a "Y" turnout and two single-slip diamonds. Note also the full range of signals

The use of such finely modelled track puts tighter restrictions on the laying and operation of rolling stock, but the effect of modelling main line railways is nearer to reality if that is your wish. We have mentioned previously the differences between gauge 1 and G scale models, but generally speaking this track suits gauge 1 better. But all worlds are possible in garden railways.

BULLHEAD TRACK
This track is available in brass or nickel silver in one-yard lengths, on plastic-based track. Because of tight tolerances, it may be necessary to remove the web where the wheel flanges could foul them if you run G scale on these tracks. Wooden-sleepered track is also available with sleepers supplied in packs of 30 or 100 - usually pre-drilled for chairs and creosoted to preserve them.

Points can be purchased ready built or in kit form, in two radii. Kits consist of numbered plastic sleepers, which can be laid out on the clearly marked template. The rails, which are pre-cut, are fixed to the chairs which are then pushed into the sleeper holes. The frog (centre section V of track) and blade (the moving portion) can be soldered or are castings. For those with very special needs for one-off points, the basic plastic parts kits are ideal, with everything except the pre-cut rails.

FLATBOTTOM TRACK
This track is available in exactly the same way and quantities as the bullhead type, i.e. plastic or wood-sleeper varieties.

10mm SCALE TRACK AND G SCALE TRAIN OPERATION
As mentioned above, certain provisoes attach to the use of 10mm scale track systems such as Tenmille products. Modern LGB rolling stock should give no problems, but this is not the case with earlier models.

Since LGB appeared in the mid 1960s no less than three flange sizes have been used. The first two would definitely need to be skimmed down in a lathe, or drill chuck and file. Locomotive standards have never changed for the driving wheels and do not appear to give trouble. However, the same cannot be said for the pony-truck wheels on 2-6-2T and 0-6-2T locomotives. These wheels are also manufactured in very hard brass, which takes considerable expertise to turn down in a lathe. Alternatively, new pony-truck wheels of later profile can be bought from the spares list.

LGB rolling stock disc wheels have the same problem, showing mostly when traversing points. The only other wheel and flange problem occurs with Bachmann, where the flanges equate to LGB's middle period, and you may have trouble when shunting over points.

4
Track Bases

Second only in importance to the selection and planning of the tracks is the decision on the type of track base necessary to carry your railway. There are many kinds of track base and every garden railway has its own pet idea and patent system. We can therefore only hope to offer a sampling of the more common developments that have taken place in the recent boom in garden railway construction.

The simplest base would probably be a patio or terrace. Many people have laid railways in such places, but unless it is a reasonably large patio and the railway is integrated, the installation is not considered to be too permanent. The aim of this book is to show how one can easily and enjoyably build a more permanent railway into or around the garden environs. It should in no way detract from the garden but should improve it through movement and added interest.

Probably the easiest method of forming a track base is simply to dig a trench in the ground some four inches deep, sprinkling some weed killer into the bottom. Now line the trench with polythene sheet. You can obtain black sheet two feet wide in rolls. Punch drainage holes at random and fill the lined trench with suitable chippings of ballast. A size of around 5-6mm is somewhat overscale but is preferable to smaller sizes of foundation which move about and get spread all over the garden. Track can be laid straight onto this ballast and held in place by skewers down into the ground (coat hanger wire is best).

A better method still is to insert bricks or blocks into the ballast and wriggle them to the required height and level with your board and spirit level. Brass screws go straight into soft blocks, or drill and plug bricks. Soft insulating building blocks let into the ground can form a base on their own too. Concrete is a more permanent base and is particularly useful in station areas which are usually much wider level places. Recent earthworks should

Trench technique track base of polythene filled with pea gravel and bricks

'Post on end' to track height and earth embankment or viaduct between

An LGB White Pass diesel passes an old time logging Shay on a line at ground level which runs from the front garden to the back garden through a storage shed built next to the garage. Notice how the driveway and a step have been accommodated by the trackbase which runs onto the lawn.

be left for a while to consolidate in the weather before engineering of the track base takes place. The trough sides can also be made of wood or aluminium lawn edging. Hardwood blocks set in concrete do not seem to work all that well because they invariably cannot accommodate changes to the track layout. They can also rot.

Concrete building blocks, not prone to water or frost damage, can also be used at ground level. A thin layer of ballast can be overlaid and the track fixed with brass screws into plugs. Screws should not project above sleeper height too much, and nothing can project above rail height. External grade PVA glue works well to fix small ballast in place. Fixing the ballast allows grass cutting with strimmers, without scattering the stones.

If cement and peat are mixed with sand, you have produced a "hypatufa" which will quickly mellow and grow green algae or moss. It is used to form artificial rocks, made by digging an irregular hole in the ground and filling with hypatufa on chicken wire framing. When set, this is uprooted and the surface is rocklike.

A somewhat older method of forming the track base, and still common with live-steam modelling, is to use well-seasoned timber soaked in creosote or other timber preservative. Be careful, some sleeper plastics are sensitive to creosote and will degrade. In the past, building sites have proven to be useful sources of suitably sized timbers. Rafters or fence posts nailed together achieve the preferred size of five and a half inches wide for single track by two inches thick.

Many garden railways are built on a base of short treated ("tantalised") timber posts sunk in the earth or concrete and then decked with 5" x 1" treated timber planks. If you infill with earth then you have an embankment. Aluminium strips or plastic edging fixed to the side forms the ballast trough. Track is laid with one-inch nails.

Where there is already a level base, perhaps crossing a path, an ideal medium is fish-tank gravel, about 2mm in size, usually brown and irregularly shaped. It can be mixed with quick setting mortar or just with ordinary cement powder which is very fine textured, then funnelled around sleepers or they can be worked down into it. Overnight damp will set the mixture.

5mm granite/limestone chips in 30 kilo bags or horticultural 6mm granite chips can be bought in largish quantities as can the fish tank gravel. A good source for the larger trough-in-the-ground ballast is builders' pea-gravel, used in quantity to ballast plastic drain pipes underground. This is 5mm plus, round in shape and can be delivered in truck load quantities for small cost. Prototype railways use sharp edged ballast because this locks in place.

To follow a curve at ground level with the trough method, then more bricks or blocks are used, or the wooden sections are cut and joined by the edging. The benefit of this system is that the whole track can be moved to a different location. Over a five year period on one system employing this type of base, only one short length needed replacing because of warping.

With a considerable investment in time and money fixed to the ground in your garden it is a good idea to consider the reusability of trackwork. Our scales are inherently much stronger than the smaller scales and take moving and relaying in their stride.

A final note - if you have the time, make foundations for the track systems a season before you commence your engineering to let everything settle. You can start one year and begin the railway the next spring for instance.

A pleasant spring day and ballasting is underway. Fish tank gravel mixed with cement powder is spooned around the sleepers then brushed into place. Overnight dew sets the mixture hard. Just in front of the ballast wagon can be a seen a magnet to activate on-board whistles and horns.

RACK RAILWAYS

These railways found all over mountainous country, for example in Switzerland, India and Wales, are basically a cog wheel meshing with toothed centre rail.

Locomotives are usually friction driven on conventional railways; they rely on their weight and the number of wheels for their friction grip on the

On the rack! The LGB Schollenen Railway locomotive climbs steeply up a rockery

rails. A 4-6-2 express locomotive might be about a hundred and forty tons weight with about eighteen tons on each of its wheels for adhesion and traction. Where steep grades occur, physical factors limit the amount of friction possible. Sometimes sand is sprayed under the wheels to improve friction but at enormous cost to the life of the railway's equipment.

To overcome these problems, a system was developed which transferred the power of the locomotive directly to a cog running on a toothed rail, fixed to the sleepers in the centre of the track. At present LGB is the only manufacturer offering a model of this system suitable for outdoor use. The plastic toothed centre rail is made in 300mm lengths and is fixed to the ordinary track by special clips which locate between the sleepers. Installation and removal are very easy.

If you are going to specialise in rack railways for your rockery or construct an area for one, note that rocks from garden centres can cost up to ten times the quarry price for large quantities. Quarries will usually deliver a part load of half to one hundredweight pieces, giving twenty to forty pieces to the ton. Two tons to four tons should start you off!

OPERATING A RACK RAILWAY

The LGB rack locomotive is capable of climbing a maximum grade of one in four (e.g. a rise of 25 units for every 100 units travelled). A somewhat lesser grade is more usual in real life however. It is well to remember that sharp curves impart more friction.

When laying rack track it is best to use the longest flexible type, particularly at the entrance and exit to the gradient or at changes in the slope. It is extremely difficult to bend shorter sections of track in the vertical direction. The use of very short sections of track does not work too well and does not look the part.

One of the problems often encountered at commencement of gradients is that rolling stock will uncouple. LGB make a coupling with a smaller uncoupling arm so that fouling of the rack is avoided. They also recommend for the safety of your passengers that hooks are fitted at both ends of carriages to avoid that most dreaded of events - the runaway carriage or wagon careering down a mountainside!

5
Garden Railway Electrics

Now that we have a clearer idea of the work involved in trackwork and track bases the next logical step is to turn to the electrics. Safety is the prime consideration with electricity out of doors. Mains power is best brought to a building such as your "engine shed", and the staff and onlookers further protected by quick blow fuses of the earth leakage type. These blow very quickly at small overloads or if an electrical short occurs. It is also good practice to fit an on/off switch at the incoming supply point to disconnect everything in an emergency or for maintenance.

TRACK ELECTRICAL SUPPLY

It is worth repeating at this stage the earlier mentioned maxim - keep it simple! This applies particularly to any electrics out of doors. The more complicated the system, the more faults can ocur and the harder they are to trace. There is also more maintenance and consequently less train running.

Again, at the risk of repetition, plan your electrical requirements. Decide where you need section breaks and isolating joints. In the real railway world a train passes from block to block and is handed from signal box to signal box. You might start with a similar plan. In our garden railway world we also have to be able to park a train and switch off its power supply while we run another activity.

The siting of blcok isolating switches in a "signal box" (garden shed) should be considered carefully. It is far better to have your switches protected from the elements, even if they are outdoor specified types. At least there is less risk of corrosion.

The low voltage power supply input to the track should use the heaviest cable possible, even mains house-wiring cable. The reason for this is simple: voltage drop, a phenomenon that is especially prevalent in garden railways

Safety is the prime consideration. The 240v mains feed is brought in overhead, suspended from a support wire at top left. The low voltage supply to track and accessories — points, lights, signals, etc — can and should also be fused. Each of the main low voltage circuits should have its own isolating switch and fuses. In the photograph, the low voltage circuits can be seen fixed to the side of the wooden track bed. Coach lighting connectors are visible between the two passenger cars. These are fed from miniature sockets at the rear of the LGB locomotive

with their long distances at low voltages. A ten metre run of 1mm cable can lose nearly two volts. Usually, 18 to 22 volts is needed at the farthest point from the supply, whether a controller or simple direct feed to the track for radio-controlled trains. Motors usually require 1.5 amps; the better quality the motor, the less the current drain. A locomotive with two motors, sound

Large amounts of heat are required to solder out of doors. A large electrical iron is needed or a portable gas iron. In the photograph an isolating joint using LGB isolators (yellow) has been formed in the up line nearest the camera. This joint also connects Tenmille track (foreground) to LGB track, in the tunnel and yet to be ballasted. It is worthwhile using a sheet of metal to shield sleepers and wood from the heat or flame

generating module, smoke generator, coach lighting and a heavy train will draw up to 5 amps.

Depending upon your isolating sections, the feed should be out along the track whenever possible. A heavy-section brass rail has greater current carrying capacity and larger cross section than any 5 amp mains cable. In

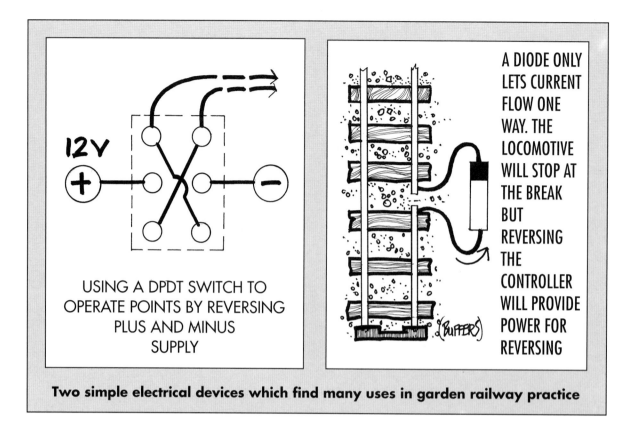

USING A DPDT SWITCH TO OPERATE POINTS BY REVERSING PLUS AND MINUS SUPPLY

A DIODE ONLY LETS CURRENT FLOW ONE WAY. THE LOCOMOTIVE WILL STOP AT THE BREAK BUT REVERSING THE CONTROLLER WILL PROVIDE POWER FOR REVERSING

Two simple electrical devices which find many uses in garden railway practice

order to use the track supply successfully, it is vital to bond all rail joints. This means soldering a jumper wire across each joint, usually the single wire from the 5 amp housewiring cable cut into short lengths. Under no circumstances should the fishplates be soldered to the rail; no expansion in warm weather or contraction in winter could occur and buckling or displacement would result. If you look at fishplates on real railway track you will see that they are greased to allow for movement of each individual piece. Rails are also electrically bonded for train detection and earthing.

Most garden railways use an 18 to 22 volt track supply with varying currents from 1 to 5 amps. This in turn requires some large transformers and controllers which are not always easy to acquire ready-made.

The size of power supply will depend very much on the size of locomotive, numer of electric motors employed, size of train and the gradients of the line. Nowadays it is possible to have a radio-controlled throttle; in effect a radio-interfaced controller, which allows the user to control the train controller remotely. This system allows maximum flexibility of working and does away with the need for long leads with controllers on the end. Power supplies for any of these systems should be indoors with only the radio controller unit outside.

Soldering requires a large soldering iron, clean track and perhaps a warm day. A 100 watt electric or gas powered blowlamp with large heat-sink soldering bit attached is best. If done carefully, the plastic sleepers will not melt but it is wise to use protection when possible. The simplest way to start is to solder wire to each piece of track before it leaves the workshop. At a later stage during laying, the leads can be attached to adjacent rails or used for power feeds. If no track bonding is carried out, ultimately fishplates which have been responsible for electrical continuity will corrode or oxidise, fill with dirt and generally fail to do the job reliably.

Certain other devices have been offered on the market, particularly in the USA in an effort to get around this problem. They usually consist of a clamp over the rail joiner and two set screws which clamp metal to metal. REA/Aristo offer their track with two screws already in the joint.

Another product that has also been called the ultimate invisible rail bonding is waxoil. This is an electrolytic oil used in the automotive industry for repelling moisture and hence maintaining good electrical contact. It has also been used by film units at sea where plugs and sockets have to be treated to prevent fast corrosion. For railway use it is suggested that the oil is diluted 50/50 with white spirit and brushed onto rail ends and fishplates then left to dry and harden for twelve hours. Provided the fishplate is a tight fit, good contact will be maintained for up to three years it is claimed.

Lehmann have recently introduced a graphite grease, which would appear to have similar properties. In the opinion of the contributors to this book however, all these systems are inferior to the soldered joint!

OVERHEAD WIRES FOR POWER SUPPLY

Catenary is the commonly used term for the overhead wiring that supplies electrical current to trams and trains, although the word catenary strictly means the supporting wires that hold the contact wire level between the successive poles or masts. The masts are usually made of treated steel, but can be concrete or timber. Attached to these are arms hanging out over the track, which support the contact wire carrying the current to be drawn by the tram or locomotive. This wire is hung from the catenary wire by insulators. There is one last component to this system; the catenary supports the contact wire by short "dropper" wires along its length.

There are several types of catenary, but the one we are concerned with here is "simple" catenary, used widely on continental electrified narrow gauge railways and tramway systems.

The variation called "trolley wire" is contact wire without the supporting catenary and is used primarily on tramway systems where the speeds are low and masts are close enough together to prevent sagging becoming too serious. Some electrified narrow gauge railways also use trolley wire, notably the Montreux Oberland Bernois line in Switzerland.

G scale modellers are fortunate that LGB have produced both catenary

(Left) Part of the demonstration layout at Garden Railway Specialists showing the excellent catenary construction

(Above) June in the garden. The cutting is formed from vertical stones set into concrete

(Below) Scratch-built Swiss locomotive and catenary

and trolley wire systems. Other manufacturers are beginning to provide us with rolling stock as well.

LGB CATENARY

It has to be said that this is an expensive system, but it does look very real. The main component is a mast in aluminium incorporating a plastic base that clips to LGB track. The mast has two support arms, for the catenary and the contact wires respectively. Catenary wire is figure-of-eight section, like the prototype, so that dropper arms can clip neatly to the waisted section without interfering with the smooth running of the locomotive's collection pantograph. The contact wires slide into brass connecting blocks at each mast.

A special version of the mast is available with a swivel base to keep it vertical on the steep gradients of the rack railway system.

TROLLEY WIRE

For this system, which is much cheaper than the catenary, LGB make sturdy but realistic grey plastic lattice-style masts. These clip to the LGB track. Each mast has a stainless steel bow-shaped arm to which is fitted the brass connecting block. In many ways this system looks as effective as catenary as it is less cluttered.

Although the systems are weatherproof, it is a good idea to remove the contact wire in winter to keep it clean and to avoid damage.

PROTOTYPICAL PRACTICE

The LGB catalogue shows the overhead contact wire curving to follow a curved track. Whilst this keeps the wire central on the pick-up surface of the pantograph, it is not really accurate. Full-sized railways keep the wire straight between each mast. This means that on curved track the masts are closer together to prevent the wire slipping off the end of the pantograph. The effect of following the prototype is very rewarding visually when the rolling stock is on the move, and it also means more even wear across the contact slider of the pick-up.

HOME MADE OVERHEAD

Joiner blocks made from brass tube and Peco rail joiners for 00 gauge combined with 00 gauge rails upside down make ideal overhead supply components. This rail is rigid enough to be used in metre lengths on straight track, thus saving on the number of masts.

6
Battery Radio Control

The newcomer may find it worthwhile to take a closer look at the possibilities of radio control. The type of set commonly used for garden railways is the two-function variety, designed for use with model boats and cars. The set consists of a transmitter, receiver, two servos and a battery box with switch. The complete outfit is small enough to fit into the space that we have at our disposal in most scale rolling stock, and the transmitter works well over the quite small distances in our garden operations.

The transmitter is the hand-held controller which sends the control signals in coded form to the receiver. It has two sticks - one moves up and down to control speed and direction, the other moves left and right, usually for the steering, but in our case to control the whistle or horn or the live steamer's reversing gear.

The receiver is the size of a matchbox and has sockets for the servo leads and battery box. It also has a length of trailing wire which is the aerial. The job of the receiver is to pick up the signals from your transmitter and, after decoding, pass them onto the servos as instructions for action.

The battery box usually holds four small 1.5 volt batteries to power the receiver and servos. With the electrical power available to us we do not always need these batteries.

The servo plugged into the receiver is about half as big again as the receiver itself. Its case contains some circuitry and a powerful miniature motor with gears. Attached to the output shaft is an arm or disc which operates whatever functions we may need, from pulling/pushing a lever to operating a microswitch and relay which in turn can operate several functions via its own connections.

Installation in electrically-powered models is different because there are no mechanical controls as on a live steam locomotive. No servos are required

Like many established lines, this one operates battery-powered radio-controlled locomotives as well as (left) conventional track controllers. To the right is a radio-controlled "interface" controller worked by the transmitter outside. At the far right is the intercom and block controller

and an electronic speed controller is used instead. This plugs into the receiver instead of a servo but has no moving parts. There are mechanical speed controllers that are operated by a servo but they are very coarse in operation. Most electronic speed controllers, following model car practice, have a "battery eliminator" which powers the receiver from the main power supply.

There are two wavebands legally available for "surface" models in the UK - 27MHz and 40MHz FM. Model aircraft users are not permitted to use the 40MHz band but can use 27MHz as well as their own exclusive 35MHz band. 27MHz is prone to interference from many sources, such as CB radio and cheap radio-controlled toys, and there are only six frequencies within the band for everyone.

40MHz is the exclusive surface model user's band. The specification placed upon manufacturers is high as are the demands of this special group of users for racing cars and boats as well as our growing band of railwaymen. There is good interference rejection and a total of thirty frequencies, so you are unlikely to be in conflict with another user.

To select or change a frequency the transmitter (Tx) and receiver (Rx) each have a small plug-in crystal (Xtal); these come in pairs and are simly unplugged and replaced. They cost only a few pounds and it is always advisable to keep a spare pair of a different frequency. The frequency being used is denoted by a small coloured ribbon attached to your transmitter aerial for 27MHz band but this is not practicable for the 30 frequencies in the 40MHz.

When running at home there is no need to worry about frequencies unless you have neighbours who are also enthusiasts or race model cars and boats. All of the components mentioned here come with simple plugs and sockets and join together at once to put you in business.

LGB tramcar adapted for radio-control. All the radio-equipment is housed in the trailer car

The usual power supply in conjunction with radio control is Ni-Cad rechargeable cells but with a sixteen to eighteen volts requirement the power pack must be substantial and will take up space in the locomotive body, tender or wagon. Ideal for the purpose are LGB's 2095 Diesel, the Mallet, REA/Aristo FA1 Diesel, the Lionel Hudson, Delton Railbus, and Bachmann 4-6-0. These also have space for a sound generator circuit and small loudspeaker.

A number of specialists exist who will convert your motive power to radio operation and for smaller power needs there are units on the market that have all the components fitted into a box van and connected to the locomotive via its lighting output sockets. This has the advantage of running any locomotive plugged into it, and easy charging or continuous running with two (while recharging takes place). It is necessary to remove track pick-ups or with many products to switch them off with a switch already fitted.

Among the wide variety of alternatives and mixes available for radio control there is a hybrid system where the track is fed a steady current from the powerful transformer - say, six amps at twenty volts - and the locomotive is controlled by wandering radio transmissions. There are still the disadvantages of dirty track and poor contact. However, a further modification has been the radio control of a track feeding controller in the "engine shed" with similar results.

With the advent of the new 40MHz sets, radio control for garden railways has become a serious challenge to conventional two-rail electric power. It overcomes almost all of the old proboems with reliability, even in tricky locations such as tunnels or indoor sections, an especial advantage with live steam which was liable to run away on occasion.

So, one can either follow a train around the track, driving it like a real engineman, or in a spirit of true decadence, relax in the deck chair waiting for the arrival of the 10.45 with a gin and tonic and ice in the box car. With garden railways all things are possible!

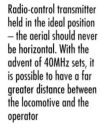

Radio-control transmitter held in the ideal position – the aerial should never be horizontal. With the advent of 40MHz sets, it is possible to have a far greater distance between the locomotive and the operator

7
Live Steam

What is it about a live steam engine that makes such an impact on people? Men, women and children who express no real interest in trains will stop to watch a steam engine go by. Thousands of people flock to steam centres and to watch steam special events. Countless books and articles have attempted to analyse the attraction, and one of the essential points seems to be that although a steam engine is only a piece of machinery it appears to have life.

Heat, fire, steam, movement, rhythmic noises and even that unforgettable smell are all ingredients of a magic concoction that brings a tingle to anyone with the memory of steam in their soul. Part of this memory and love for steam engines is what makes many of us want to recreate our own railway world in miniature.

In the smaller scales most modellers have no option but to represent steam engines in visual outline only, but of necessity the wheels have to be powered by an electric motor hidden inside. However beautiful, these models always lack the essential ingredient. They are not self sustaining, generating their own power from fire and water.

Smoke on a summer's day – the sound, smell and atmosphere of live steam propulsion is something that cannot be equalled

By moving to the larger garden scales we give ourselves the option of running real steam engines. There is a vast range of models available which operate just like the real thing. There are fewer models that actually burn coal and, because relatively more expertise is required to drive them, they are definitely not for the beginner. The use of gas or methylated spirit provides an acceptable substitute.

The garden railway enthusiast must be sure of what he wants from a railway and its locomotives before embarking on what may be an expensive mistake. The prospective purchaser of a steam locomotive should ask the following questions:

● Do I want an instant train service, turned on and off at short notice?
● Do I want to operate a number of trains simultaneously?
● Am I more interested in complex shunting operations than watching trains running?
● Do I have a line which is very short, or end-to-end, or with sharp curves or steep gradients?

If the answer to most of these is "yes", then you will be well satisfied with two rail-electric operation and steam is probably not for you.

The other side of the coin however, needs to be examined:

● Do you like the idea of operating or driving a real steam locomotive?
● Are you attracted by the sight and sound and smell of real steam, as distinct from electronic sound and synthetic smoke?
● Do you like the idea of preparing a steam locomotive for a run and the operations involved in its care?
● Do you also like the idea of getting to know your locomotive and learning to judge its capabilities under different operating conditions?

A yes to any of these questions and you are a potential convert to live steam and an engine driver!

With the decision to buy live steam you will need to seek advice about your choice. EVERY locomotive is an individual, there are many types and there are options for manual or radio control. There is no substitute for seeing locomotives in action and using the opportunity to talk things over with enthusiasts. Make contact with a local group and go along on an open day. Written advice will always contain personal preferences but there are a number of points worth bearing in mind.

Most model steam locomotives are virtually hand made and this does not come cheaply. You can however buy a reliable, powerful, locomotive for about the same price as a factory-built top-of-the-range electric model. Because of its low cost, many people begin their career with the humble British Mamod. These are excellent value but severely limited in

(Opposite top)
Live steam can give superb smoke effects, especially in cold weather

(Opposite bottom)
Elsa rumbles across an impressive girder bridge with steam to spare

Atlantic, a chunky live-steam model of an Andrew Barclay 0-6-2 tank

performance in terms of power, slow running ability and duration of run. There are several upgrading conversions for different burners and radio control.

The first locomotive that you purchase should really be a soundly engineered product from one of the established manufacturers. Even their basic locomotives will give many years of satisfactory service and pleasure and probably keep their monetary value as well.

CYLINDERS AND VALVES

The simplest system for converting steam pressure to rotary motion of the wheels is by oscillating cylinders like those on the Mamod. Reversal of these engines is by a rotary valve which also controls the steam quantity and hence the speed. A feature of these cylinders is that they are more efficient at high speeds and so are not so suitable for slow speed narrow gauge locomotives.

Engines with piston valves can be reversed with a simple rotary valve whereas engines with slide valves need valve gear to change direction. The simplest form of valve gear is slip-eccentric and, although this is very reliable, to reverse a locomotive it must be pushed a short distance in the direction of travel to set the gear.

Effective reversing gear comes in many shapes and, in principle, a lever in the cab operates rods which set the valves and determine the direction of travel. The various systems, named after their inventors and common in model form, include Hackworth, Stephenson and Joy, with Walschaerts the most widely used valve gear.

The performance of locomotives with complex but efficient valve gear

A superb Roundhouse model of a Baldwin 2-6-2 built in 1919 for the Sandy River Railroad. The water tank has a pump in the tender, so that by topping up the gas the locomotive can be kept in steam as long as desired

The ultimate model locomotive! Built by Hugh Saunders, *Quicksilver* is coal-fired and has full Walschaert's valve gear, axle-driven water pump, mechanical lubricator and whistle. The prototype is to be found on the Darjeeling Himalaya Railway

such as Walschaerts under radio-control is very close to real life, with satisfactory sounds and steady increases in speed pulling heavy loads away from stations and up gradients.

BOILERS AND BURNERS

Effective steam generation in a steam locomotive is the most important factor for consideration, whatever its size. If it cannot make enough steam, it

Frank S, a unique live steam collaboration between LGB and Aster

will not move. In the prototype, the heat to boil water comes from coal or oil; in models oil is a non starter and coal boilers are expensive to build and need great skill to operate successfully. Most model boilers are therefore gas or methylated spirit fired. It must be made clear that engines cannot be run on gas or meths but that some models are offered with options for either.

Meths-fired engines are usually pot-boilers which have wicks below the boiler like a kettle. They are simple to operate but their performance can suffer in wind and rain unless the fire is well shielded with a firebox and side tanks. Gas-fired engines usually burn bottled butane in a blowlamp type flame pointing down the centre of a single flue tube in the boiler. Steam can be raised very quickly and the engine can be run in all weathers.

Some more expensive engines use more complex Smithies or fire-tube boilers which have meths or gas burners in a firebox. The fire is drawn through the boiler by the exhaust steam from the cylinders which is directed up the chimney. Initial steam raising on engines with this type of boiler must be achieved with a small electrically-powered fan inserted in the chimney which draws the fire. After about five minutes there should be sufficient steam in the boiler for the engine's own steam blower to take over and the battery blower can then be removed. Operation of an engine with an internally-fired boiler is far more like driving a full-sized engine and, although rather complex for a beginner, it can be very rewarding to learn the skills necessary to get the best performance from an engine pulling a heavy train.

Some gas burners can be quite noisy but can be adjusted to produce as much steam as required for a load. Refuelling can be difficult, particularly in cold weather which affects the gas pressure. There are also safety aspects which must be respected when handling bottled gases, although it must be said that all live steam operations should involve a healthy respect of burning fuel, boiling water and pressures up to 75lbs psi.

In these few pages it has not been possible to deal with all the aspects of steam locomotive purchase and operations. Whether you opt for a gas-fired locomotive with full radio control on the regulator and reverse, or a simple manual slip-eccentric meths-fired pot-boiler, as you strike the first match you will open up a whole new world of activity in your garden and beyond.

David Pinniger's Ambledown Valley Railway in 1981. Note on the left the small conifer just planted and also the new building. The track is on 4in x 1in timber and the grass embankment has yet to be built up. The locomotives are an Archangel "Sgt Murphy" and "Snowdon Ranger" on the bridge

The same location eight years later. Note the growth of the central conifer and the building now shaded by trees. The visiting "Sgt Murphy" is owned by John Chalmers

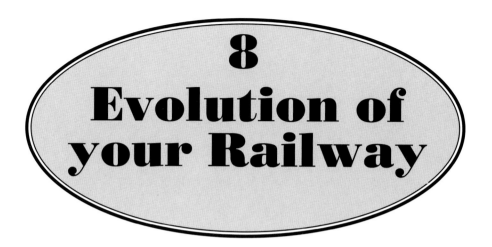

8
Evolution of your Railway

Every newly constructed railway has a raw and unrealistic look. How long it will take for the railway to mature and blend in with its surroundings depends upon the materials used and how you go about adding character.

A new oval of track laid directly onto a concrete patio with plastic buildings and pot plants will always look like an indoor train set moved outside. A little extra effort and thought will enable the train set boundaries and limitations to be eliminated and make your railway a part of the garden and outside world. In the section on track bases we drew attention to the importance of choosing the right methods and materials. These not only determine the initial character but the possibilities and potential for making changes as the railway evolves.

Ballast immediately places the track visually as part of the scene, and eliminates the impression of rails laid on the ground. A coat of matt brown to the rail sides removes the newness, though they will weather in a short time anyway. Keep the rail top running surfaces clean at all times.

It is important to keep fresh soil away from the immediate vicinity of the track otherwise nature soon takes over and trains will be derailed by the jungle growth. Vegetation will only add to the overall effect when it is controlled and grows where you determine. Keep a barrier between the track ballast and the garden proper to minimise any visual intrusion.

Cement blocks used as a track base will weather eventually but can be helped with liquid manure to encourage algae growth, as can new rocks. Grass can be taken quite close to the track. It should be quite simple to construct a weed killer train from tank wagons to spray the track and ballast.

The fine-bladed varieties of hard-wearing grass tend to look much better than the broad-leaved varieties that also creep. The track base can be extended outwards with alpine chippings in various colours. Together with

some spreading alpines a season's growth should see the railway blend in perfectly.

Visual disguise of elevated timbers can be made using rock, grass embankments or box hedging with its small leaves. Privet too fits this category. Walls, fences and garden rubbish can become eyesores against the near perfection of your growing miniature world. A photograph will often direct your attention to a feature that you have become accustomed to but need to see in a new light.

Bridges are usually so beneficial in setting the scale that it is difficult to have too many. They should appear to have a purpose and give sufficient

A busy scene on a newly-constructed rockery layout. Pola provide the station and signal box, Aristo the watchtower and LGB the small girder bridge. Compare this with the same layout in the "Getting Started" section – note the track is now ballasted

Bird's-eye view (above) and side elevation of an American-style trestle bridge. In the lower picture it is being crossed by an LGB White Pass & Yukon Railroad diesel

clearance for the largest possible locomotive. USA "Old Timers" with wood burning smoke stacks and cabooses need the full height of the loading gauge.

Even a simple wooden pedestrian bridge can be very effective , stirring childhood memories of trains passing beneath. It is perfectly feasible to make a wooden bridge from square section hardwood, waterproof glue and tiny nails in a working day. The materials are in every Do-It-Yourself shop now.

Bridges which support the railway can be impressive too, even when simply constructed.

To avoid disaster remember that locomotives can weigh over ten pounds, and some of the big live steamers much more. Make sure that there is a strong plank or angle iron (from garden centres) or even a concrete window lintel to form the structural base of the bridge, or keep the span short and go for multiples. Much more elaborate girder bridges can be made from small section metal angle or plastic track; even small section plastic drainpipes can be welded into bridges with the proper glue and imagination.

A suspension bridge could be made using square section drainpipe for the uprights and motor cycle chains as the suspension means with a single track deck up to six feet in span. It has been done.

Concrete bridges cast in situ on a hardboard framework can be quite elegant. Concrete always needs chicken wire mesh embedded inside for strength.

If you look closely at real bridges you will see that they are all supported on pads or hinges to allow for movement when loads pass over. Your bridges should fit the gap

A diesel-hauled train winds its way along the edge of the garden path. The same stretch of line is shown under construction on page 23

that they are spanning and appear to be supported at the ends in the same way. Modern welded steelplate bridges can be modelled from sheet plastic and bridge construction is also the basis for turntables.

Both small and large plastic bridges are available from LGB and there are components made of stone, aluminium and wood in kit form from many suppliers. Concrete viaducts are a real challenge, and they need proper engineering skills exactly as used in the building of real railways. The ground on which they are built must be stable, good "footings" (foundations) will be needed and the ends must abut to the terrain without the possibility of movement under the track. Mistakes are hard to rectify!

Footings for bridges in ponds can be tricky and a good solution is to place a thick sheet of polystyrene on the bottom and build on it or, if you have a very large pond, a floating centre can be made using a block of polystyrene.

A further use for bridges is that they can disguise lift-out sections,

Simple catenary using LGB masts and upside-down Peco 00 nickel-silver rail. The spans are from brass wire

perhaps where the line crosses a path. The main problem is electrical continuity. You cannot rely on normal fishplates. An electrical feed wire to the section and hidden wire continuing to the next section leaves only the problem of rail alignment. Strength is essential because of wear and tear.

While bridges and embankments add variety and life to the developing railway, they are potential danger points in case of derailments. To prevent valuable stock or locomotives plunging three feet or so to the ground, some form of retention is needed. This can be as simple as a check-rail which is laid next to the running rail but inside the two rails. This keeps the wheels roughly in the track space even if bumping over the sleepers. You will see them in pointwork.

Parapet walls in various heights made of reconstituted stone, and foam plastic are available, or you can model and cast your own. Low fences can be made from wire strung between little wooden posts or sleepers. Be careful that the fence itself cannot inflict damage to the stock.

Fences are extremely difficult to model convincingly because true to scale would be so fragile while robust fencing can look like a prison perimeter. Pola and others supply plastic fencing which needs to be toned down on installation.

Cuttings we have mentioned earlier but they serve as an excuse for an "overbridge" over the line. Cuttings also flood so provide drainage! Visually they can be disappointing but, where there is scope for rapid changes in levels, there is no doubt that the sight of a train leaving a short tunnel and then running through a cutting and onto an embankment is difficult to equal.

Cuttings also provide protection from the wind. Trains have been known to derail in strong gusts. Heed the warning of the windgauge sited on the Owencarrow viaduct after the 1905 disaster!

9
Giving Your Railway Its Own Character

Does your developing railway tend to look like all the others you have seen? Is the stock, like theirs, straight from the catalogue? If you are a true collector, or reproducing a particular line from manufactured items and your intention is to collect one example of each item boxed and mint, then this section is not for you.

However, if you want to create your own distinctive railway, with its own unique identity, you can achieve this with a little thought and effort. There is a dilemma in that you have just paid a great deal of money for an engine or coach and do not want to risk spoiling it or lowering its value. The answer is to start small with items that are cheap, secondhand or well used already. We have previously mentioned Playmobil, the favourite for repainting with enamel or modifying with a small modellers' saw and ABS glue. The model railway and war game diorama magazines often feature weathered models and "how to do it" features.

The Bachmann range can easily be "improved" with silver applied to wheel rims with a paint pen from the model car range and Playmobil disassembly and respraying is a simple customising exercise. If you are experienced or careful, LGB itself will reward an imaginative conversion. Many locomotives such as Beyer Garratts have been fashioned from LGB components.

If you have a narrow gauge line in the making, and you are building a miniature version of a favourite prototype, then there are specialist books and societies for your guidance.

There are many transfer lettering sheets available and spray cans of enamel paint. From the automotive industry, plastic body filler is a most useful modelling material and the perfect adhesive for metals and some plastics. It also works out of doors when you wish to fix a signal or building permanently to concrete or rock. A unique product, Milliput, sticks to all

Appleyard Station with rolling stock and motive power almost entirely home-built. The Garratt in the foreground is typical of many such locomotives on the railway which began life as LGB moguls. The buildings are permanent and are covered by boxes in bad weather

plastics and metal, and can be moulded before it sets hard.

Most manufacturers produce beautiful models which are often close to scale replicas of the real locomotives, coaches or wagons. LGB for example makes models of the rolling stock of fifty different railways, much of which did not run together and was also different gauges. The important thing is that you make the rules on your railway and you are free to do what you want. It is often the case however that some things do not look right when run together for reasons of size, style or colour.

Manufacturers have a tendency to paint things with a very bright glossy finish or leave bright coloured plastic which is intended to appeal to the potential buyer. One look at most working railways, even preserved ones, shows that very soon the coaches and wagons acquire a patina of work use. Take care that paints are compatible with the plastic and avoid cellulose-based automotive paints - they will dissolve most existing paint and some plastics too!

The secret of good painting is in the masking off. Masking tapes and newspaper can take a long time to arrange, and a quick pass with the paint spray lasts just a few seconds, but the trouble is worth the finish. Use light coats, let them dry and build up colour. If you are attempting to weather stock to make it appear more realistic, study real photographs and magazines which feature weathered model trains.

There are several metal replica paints from brushed aluminium to gun metal, ideal for couplings and massive locomotive castings such as pony trucks. Almost never use matt black on its own, even coal dust is grey and gloss black.

One feature that really creates a railway identity and character is having your own railway name. One or two well known modellers have christened their lines with names such as "Lake George & Boulder" to fit the LGB initials. In most cases it will mean removing the original painted or transferred letters with a wet scraper blade or wet and dry sand paper as used for car body repairs. Careful matching of colours can allow you simply to paint over the whole area with base colour. This is more preferable where there is rivet detail.

There is a great deal of press-on lettering available for model railways

A level crossing set in concrete. The check rails are formed from LGB rail

Chemin de fer Ardennais, the freelance metre gauge main line of David Edgley, set in the Ardenne region – well, in an English garden really! David's philosophy has been to create a credible "what might have been" scenario by designing and building a layout with a definate purpose as well as its own corporate identity. Not only with liveries, but unique stock. The picture on this page shows a heavily rebuilt U-25B American diesel, while opposite No68, a freelance design, takes a freight around the lake

and even the possibility of your own specially made sheets now exists. Nameplates in brass with locomotive names or your railway motif are comparatively very cheap and easy to obtain through specialist dealers. Another valuable aid for those using waterslide transfers is a softener which makes the transfer fit snugly over rivets and to planking. Decal-set is one such product. Always cover lettering with a thin coat of matt or satin clear coating to delay the onset of wear and tear effects.

The ultimate way to create your own railway corporate identity is totally to repaint the stock in your own colours with a distinct house livery for coaches, wagons and locomotives. The American railroads, more than the European ones, used to paint their crack express trains in special liveries. You could run just one train in your own special chosen livery and keep your day to day railway operations for common stock straight from the catalogue. The "Daylights", West Coast USA expresses in various colours - mostly black orange and brown or red, "The Blue Train" of South Africa and "Silver Jubilee" are all examples.

Avoid high gloss if you are going to embark upon this road and dismantle as much as possible before painting. Study automotive repair techniques for custom painting. With professional lettering and light weathering your railway will truly come alive.

Avoid lining engines and coaches yourself; even the press-on lines are difficult to attach properly to detailed scale models. Weathering will not disguise a poor paint job but make it worse. The most effective weathering is applied to a really good finish.

You are now ready to grab a hacksaw and start "kit bashing". You can remove or super detail as you wish to emphasise your corporate image. Again, start with simple change and follow photographs or specialist magazines for detailed headlights, cab roofs, ventilators or steps. "Plasticard" sheets are marvellous for adding detail or complete rebuilds. They come in all sizes and thicknesses, clear and white or black, with detailed surfaces such as planks, or smooth. Experience with this material and plastic sections such as girders, or rods and tubes, will lead you on to bigger things such as buildings and even to scratchbuild rolling stock or locomotives.

10 Accessories

There seem to be two schools of thought regarding the incorporation of buildings into the garden scenery. There are those who add one or two important structures such as a station or signal box, and those who accumulate whole villages populated with very active little people engaged in all sorts of industry as well as working on the railway. Luckily there are products to suit the most dedicated developer.

BUILDINGS AND PEOPLE

Some of the most useful buildings come from Pola, which are those used in the LGB catalogue illustrations. Pola buildings come as simple glue-together kits because they would need such large shipping boxes if assembled. They are heavy duty plastic and quite real from a short distance. As well as the station buildings there are many other kits including farm and circus buildings and "specials" such as limited edition working windmills and sawmills. The water towers that work to replenish locomotives or their drivers with something stronger are very popular.

A growing number of firms are producing stone and terracotta buildings, either as kits or hand-finished cottages and lineside structures. There are also terracotta people for distant viewing. All of the buildings mentioned this far can be lighted from a twelve to eighteen volt supply, and some produce smoke from their chimneys using the same mechanism as the locomotives where a special oil (also a track cleaner fluid!) is heated by a hot wire. There are even different kinds of smoke - puffs or a stream.

Playmobil, though toy-like, have kit buildings and little people in a host of activities, a wonderful way of introducing children to our small world. The most impressively detailed figures come from Preiser, but LGB and others have painted figures of acceptable quality.

Station platforms, not always used on the continent and in some of the USA, can be formed from concrete poured into a make-shift mould about 3/4 inch high, then painted with roofing bitumen for tarmac. Leave a good gap for rolling stock overhang. True to scale means platforms up to fifteen feet long at termini so we tend to model wayside halts and country stations.

Figures by Preiser and LGB wait at the Pola station. The water tower and coaling depot are Pola. Playmobil provided the wagon loads and grey isolating switch at centre. Ballast by Garden Railway Specialists

MISCELLANEOUS ACCESSORIES

What else could we call this section? - we needed a "catch-all" for some of the things which did not fit neatly elsewhere and we needed to draw your

More activity on the Michaelmas Line, which extensively features hand-built South African locomotives and carriages

attention to the enormous range of garden bits and pieces now coming on the market. Our hobby, which is truly international, is as well served as the traditional small indoor scales. A browse through any of the major catalogues or back numbers of garden railway magazines will reveal all.

To whet your appetite and assist with the decision of which way to go with your own railway style, a look around the shelves of a major garden railway specialist produced the following choice items at random:

A watchtower signal box - the cabin is high up between two tracks, it has smoke from the stove and switched lights. Needs a "fat controller" as occupant. The windows open and so do the two storage boxes at the trackside.

A set of level crossing lights with sounding bells which are activated as a train approaches in the USA.

Wagon loads, in large polythene bags - barrels, boxes, cases, oil drums.

Electronic auto-shuttle to make the train go backwards and forwards automatically; one with full control of acceleration and duration, one simpler and built into a buffer stop.

Station lamps, road vehicles (modern or vintage), sound units for steam, diesel.

Signals - electric working, manual, coloured lights, gantries.

Station furniture, fences (metal pattern or wooden) by the yard.

Stone structures in component form, arches, pillars, tunnel mouths.

Newcomers need have no fears that there are insufficient accessories and equipment available. The range is probably greater than in some other gauges.

High Pringle station on the Loss Gill Beck Railway consists entirely of buildings from the
Pola range of kits. A limited-edition LGB Mozambique Railways' Garratt is awaiting
its next turn of duty

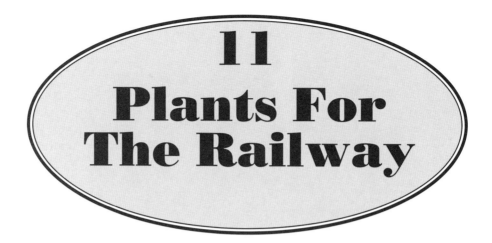

11
Plants For The Railway

To many people the garden may be as important as the railway they are creating within it. The reason that garden matters do not occupy half this book is simply because of the wealth of botanical and horticultural information and also the readily available expertise in books and magazines.

Having a railway in the garden gives the avid gardener even more niches and different planting habitats with which to experiment, which is as good a reason as any for starting a garden ralway project. When considering plants for the miniature railway scenery, it is obviously important to think small, not only in height and spread of plant, but also in leaf size.

Probably the most important task when "greening" the railway is to give some structure, using miniature trees. There are numerous dwarf conifers and evergreens which provide all-the-year colour and interest. It is vital

A pleasing variety of plants add greatly to the charm of this G Scale line. The battery-powered diesel locomotive has speed and reverse controls on the roof

A single track line and the LGB steam tram enhance a lovely garden in Buckinghamshire on a rare summer's day

when selecting your trees to check carefully that they are the dwarf and not just slow-growing varieties. When choosing, consider the size of the leaves for proportion, spreading habit (if any), rate of growth and overall shape. Some specimens can be made more tree-like (hence less shrub-like) by removing the lower branches and revealing a trunk.

Shrubs such as Box (Buxus) and Lonicera nitida can be used and trimmed to create miniature trees or hedges. Cuttings of these are easy to

Plant effects in winter can be just as striking as in the summer months. Note the snowplough on the locomotive

take and grow quickly into more of the same. Use any clippings as your cuttings.

There are also some miniature flowering shrubs which can enhance a railway. Some of the Hebes are excellent, with small leaves, flowers and compact growing habit. They vary in colour and shape of foliage so choose carefully. Some Potentillas can be kept trim and provide colour with small dog-rose shaped blooms all summer. They have tiny narrow leaves, but with the disadvantage of being leafless during the winter.

For those fortunate enough to have an acid soil, dwarf azaleas can look like stunning full-sized rhododendrons to the passengers on your railway.

Miniature roses, especially the ground cover varieties, can also be effective. Euonymus varieties, if kept in trim, can provide welcome evergreen variegated foliage to act as a foil to often shorter-lived flowering plants.

Heathers are versatile plants and can be found in a wide selection of foliage colour from yellow to deep blue-green, which may also vary through the seasons. However, these must be selected carefully as many cannot tolerate limey soils. If in doubt about your soil or if you have imported soil from your engineering works, use a pH tester from the garden centre.

With limey alkaline soil, your choice of heathers will be limited to the winter flowing Ericas. If your soil is acid, then plant Erica and Calluna varieties. Once you have planted these in light, peaty soil, give them a good "haircut" after flowering to keep their shape compact. Heathers can spread quickly and can look straggly if not kept in trim.

Many alpines and plants recommended for rockeries will fit into the railway scene, especialy if they are used for growing in cracks and crevices of

Planting to good effect on an LGB layout in Germany

walls and rockery scenery. It is impossible to name here all those species which are suitable but some favourites - easily available - are described.

Try a yellow spring-flowering, grey-leaved Alyssum Montanum, growing down an embankment. This is smaller and neater than the more familiar Alyssum Saxitale. Contrast this with varieties of white or purple Arabis or Aubretia which can also be found with variegated leaves. Even when not in flower, these plants provide an attractive mound of foliage all year. Some low growing varieties of Campanula also provide this foliage, and have small bell-like flowers in summer. They have the added advantage of seeding and spreading themselves into the smallest cracks and crevices of paving and walls.

For sunny banks you cannot beat the Helianthemums which have a splendid spreading show of colour, their blooms similar to Potentilla but with the advantage of being evergreen. They also grow easily from cuttings. Other plants suitable for growing down sunny banks or for creating a spreading mound include Dianthus, Phlox (alpine variety), Saxifrages, Sedums and Sempervivums.

The Sedums are also suitable for small areas near the track and stations which might be looking bare. This varied genus is very good tempered; pieces can be uprooted and put down even where there is little soil and then soon take root and spread. Some may be invasive but can easily be controlled.

The Sempervivums are equally useful. It is best to select these carefully, rejecting the large dramatic rosetted varieties which could be more daunting

(Left)
A garden railway wholly integrated into its surroundings can give a wonderful sense of achievement. This view was taken in late evening sunshine on David Joy's Loss Gill Beck line – some 750 feet up in the Pennines!

(Above)
Another view of the same line, with an LGB steam tram awaiting departure from Loss Gill Bottoms station

than a Triffid to the small station master! These too can be uprooted. Remove a rosette, make a small hole or poke the root into a crevice and the plant will soon begin to spread, making an attractive mound of rosettes.

Herbs can also find a place on the railway and be useful for the kitchen too. Many of them have small leaves and penetrating scents. Thymes have small leaves and can vary from gold/green and silver to dark green, with tiny purple or white blossoms. When walked on or crushed the leaves release a delightful perfume, as does Camomile which is sometimes used for whole lawns and could be ideal for that railway cutting where trimming grass is impractical.

In the autumn, bulbs can be planted, but do check carefully that the plant will be in the right proportion to the railway. Find some shady corners, not too near the trackside, for miniature Daffodils, Narcissi, rockery Tulips, Crocus, Scillas and Anemone Blanda. Then in the spring you will have a blaze of colour for the first train out of the shed.

Last but not least, do not forget the annual, which can provide instant colour and cover for the new railway, and patch any gaps. Faithfuls such as white Alyssum and blue Lobelia - including the trailing varieties with yellow Tagetes - can be very effective, forming clumps of colour throughout the summer. Annuals whose larger blooms grow on taller stems look out of place and proportion with a miniature railway. If you are lucky, some annuals will self seed and save you the job the following year.

There are several ways to incorporate garden and railway, including the obvious rockery, the scree bed based upon peat and gravel, a peat wall or raised bed, a water garden with streams and a track along a dry stone wall around the garden edge.

Apart from planting out annuals at the end of May, alpines, shrubs trees and perennials are best planted in the autumn or early spring so that they can become established before the drier summer weather. Autumn is a good time to undertake railway engineering and landscaping together. You will know where the existing planting is and the ground will have consolidated so that works will not be built upon shifting ground.

The whole railway, planting and all, will blossom forth the following spring - even if steam is a little slower in coming.

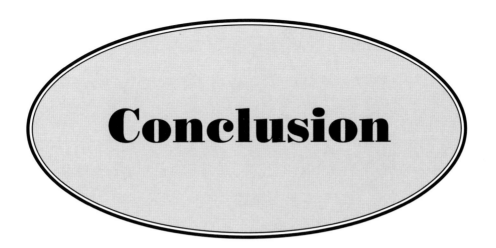

Conclusion

This book has, we hope, given you some of the basic expertise needed to build and run a garden railway. At its simplest, a circuit to provide activity and pleasure, enhancing your garden and horticultural interests. At the other end of the spectrum, you can be engineer, signalman, constructor, or tackle any job in between on a complex layout involving the whole family.

This fascinating hobby provides for outdoor activities in all weathers, and indoors through construction, electronics and that universal enjoyment - planning for the future.

GLOSSARY

Ballast. Holds track in position, allows drainage.

Battery Eliminator. Circuit to provide smaller voltage from low voltage.

Blades. Moving rails in points.

Block. A short length of track which can be isolated from the next, in the prototype with signals.

Blower. A device for creating a draught for a steam engine boiler.

Bogies. USA trucks.

Buffers. Objects fitted to locomotives, goods wagons and coaches to keep them apart and prevent damage when stock is pushed.

Buffer stop. A device at the end of tracks to prevent trains running off.

Bullhead. Figure-of-eight section rail.

Caboose. Guard's van.

Catenary. Wire between poles; supports contact wire for overhead supply.

A railway without frills can often capture the feel of the prototype than a more complex layout. This LGB Mallet appears to be threading through open country on a long single line. (Inset) A short train from Zermat drops down to lower level behind a small tree-like box shrub. The Mamod steam locomotive emerging from the tunnel belongs to the family of locomotives that

started many enthusiasts on the live steam trail. Gangers' hut in terracotta by Steamlines; tunnel mouth from Garden Railway Spaecialists

Chair. Holds rail in place on sleeper.
Couplings. Various devices used to connect vehicles together. (US couplers).
Diamond. Two tracks cross at an angle.
Fine-Scale. Close to accurate scale.
Fishplate. Rail joiner.
Flange. Raised rim of wheel which keeps the wheels on the track.
Flatbottom. Upside down T-shaped rail.
Footings. Foundations for construction.
Frog. V-section at split of points.
Gauge. The distance between the rails.
Gondola (USA). Low-sided bogie goods truck.
Hypatufa. Cement, sand, peat. Simulates rocks.
Meths. Methylated ethanol (spirits) or industrial alcohol. (This is not pure methanol).
Pilot (USA). Cowcatcher.
Pot-boiler. A simple steam engine boiler where the water is boiled from heat underneath.
Prototype. The real railways that we model.
Rack. Toothed rail between the running rails of a rack railway.
Rail bonding. To provide electrical path to the adjoining rail.
Rolling stock. Wagons, carriages (sometimes locomotives).
Section. A block.
Shoulder. Part of ballast outside the sleeper. Stops sideways movement.
Signal box. USA switch tower.
Sleepers. USA cross-ties.
Spike. Holds flat-bottomed rail on to sleepers.
Switch (USA). Points.
Switch Stand (USA). Point lever.
Switcher (USA). Small shunting engine.
Terracotta. Unglazed fired clay models.
Transformer. Voltage changing device (mains to low voltage).
Trolley wire. Simple overhead supply system, often for trams.
Turnout. Points.
Valve gear. Mechanism of rods for operating the steam valves on an engine to change direction.